# PAINTINGS, DRAWINGS AND ETCHINGS

1. Rembrandt leaning on a Stone Sill. Half-length, 1639
207 × 164 mm. Paris, Bibliothèque Nationale

# Rembrandt van Rijn

# PAINTINGS, DRAWINGS AND ETCHINGS

Selected and Introduced by
Nigel Lambourne

The Folio Society
London 1963

PRINTED IN GREAT BRITAIN
Printed and bound by Jarrold & Sons Ltd, Norwich
Set in 'Monotype' Plantin type
Printed throughout by photo-lithography

# Introduction

Against the background of painting in seventeenth-century Holland, with its trivial academic anecdotes on parochial themes, the phenomenon of Rembrandt stands out brilliantly in terms of worldliness and poetic realism.

On 15 July 1606, Rembrandt, the last but one of seven children, was born to the family of Harmensz van Rijn, a Leyden miller. From the age of six he received a moderately sound education and finally matriculated at Leyden University. Although his parents hoped he might study law, his constant preoccupation with drawing eventually persuaded them to apprentice him for three years to a dull but sound local artist, Jacob van Swanenburgh. At the end of this period another master was recommended and Rembrandt left home for the first time, the then celebrated painter, Pieter Lastman, taking him as studio assistant at his fashionable residence in Amsterdam. After a profitable year in this city he returned to Leyden where he soon began to establish a modest reputation with portraits of local businessmen and their families. Some of his first etchings were also made at this time.

Shortly after his twenty-fifth birthday he left Leyden for the last time, and by the winter of 1633 had settled into a small studio in Amsterdam. His work gradually gained a following, and the sons of prosperous families began to be apprenticed as full-time pupils in his *atelier*. It was during this period that he also met Saskia van Uylenburgh, and late in 1634 they were married.

In Holland, unlike Italy, there was little or no patronage from the Church, although wealthy and politically powerful Guilds, such as the Amsterdam Burghers, delighted in ordering large group portraits of their complacent-looking members. In spite of the many exasperating alterations often involved, Rembrandt gained valuable experience as well as financial stability from such work. His income from both pupils and sales soon encouraged him to buy a large house in the Bloemgracht quarter, and to acquire an adjacent warehouse for conversion into a more expansive workshop.

From about 1635 Rembrandt's prestige grew steadily. The relative affluence of the late 1630s fired an already extravagant temperament; Persian, Indian and Renaissance prints and drawings were continually being bargained for and purchased at high prices. Echoes and free translations of many of these works can be traced from this period through to his last years.

At the frequent art auctions held in Amsterdam, the painter's familiar bulk would leap up with such fantastically lavish bids that his resources were often strained to breaking-point. In justification he claimed that this kind of example was necessary to 'uphold the honour of art'. Pictures, fragments of armour, swords, helmets and costumes were constantly being delivered to the Bloemgrachthuis—some of these 'props' later playing their part in Old Testament designs as well as providing the models with 'character' rôles.

Rembrandt's private life with Saskia and Hendrickje Stoffels (his future mistress) has aroused a great deal of disparaging comment from those moralising zealots for whom the passionate humanity of his painting is of far less account than an apparently respectable demeanour. Undoubtedly it is true that an 'influential' citizen who called at the studio would often be curtly admonished by Rembrandt as he was disturbed at work, or a sitter would be sent away by housekeeper Hendrickje because he preferred to continue with the picture on hand. Yet for long periods he lived as frugally as a peasant on an evening meal of bread, cheese and pickled herring, rarely visiting taverns or, indeed, seeing anyone other than pupils or family. He would paint, destroy, re-draw and re-paint; as one picture became too wet for further immediate work, he would touch in another subject on a fresh canvas or panel. And all the time several etching plates might be immersed in acid, their states being watched and developed in the presence of an experienced pupil. Hendrickje, Saskia, and Rembrandt's son Titus, were all constantly called upon to act as models.

By 1642, when he painted the prodigious 'Night Watch' commission for the Civic Guard, his reputation was well established, but his household affairs were chaotic. Debt piled upon debt, and niggling alterations to pictures were frequently demanded by the patrons; all of which made him more intractable than ever. When, the end of the year, Saskia died, financial difficulties increased unmercifully.

In an attempt to offset the heavy percentage now claimed by creditors on every picture he sold, Hendrickje Stoffels and Titus formed a partnership as art dealers and agents for his work. But the firm met with little success; the profits from sales were seldom enough to meet outstanding debts.

By 1650 the dramatic power of Rembrandt's work was being noticed abroad but in Holland, during the middle years of the century, a popular taste for artificial classicism and slick academic techniques took root. Rembrandt's reputation began to wither. The broad, vigorous handling and uncompromising approach to his subjects became largely unsaleable.

In the winter of 1656 he was publicly declared insolvent. Once again he appeared at an auction, this time of his own house and its entire contents—the superb collection of prints and drawings as well as all the finished paintings in the studio.

Some public commissions were still to come, among them the large 'Staalmeesters' group for the Syndics of the Cloth Hall in 1662, but, although this was relatively well paid work, it did little to alleviate his utter poverty and declining health. Alone, and already largely forgotten, he died in a small Amsterdam apartment house on 4 October, 1669.

During the last seven years of his life, in spite of illness and failing sight, he produced some of the most powerful studies of interpretative sympathy ever seen in European painting—a deeply moving reflection of poetry and compassion through which he also achieved the great transition from an environment of a dying classical idealism to a highly individual realism. In so doing he anticipated terms of expression as far forward as Delacroix and even the early years of our own century.

# Contents

# Paintings

Few painters have revealed so much of their personality in their work as Rembrandt. In modern terms, he can be studied both as a compassionate analyst and as an uncompromising realist.

No one has possessed a greater power for raising a subject above its illustrative content to the highest levels of imaginative story-telling, always free from mere anecdote or trivial impression. 'A Woman Bathing' (16) is typical of this power. A peasant-like woman is wading in a deep pool, yet the dignity of her movement—the utter simplicity of her gesture holding up her shift—is conveyed in the broadest of tones, restrained in colour and timeless in impact.

Rembrandt's models frequently reflect their humble origin; they are seldom disguised even when a drama of classical dimensions is the theme. In both etched and painted versions of the 'Descent from the Cross' Rembrandt portrayed himself as a fascinated and horror-stricken assistant; the Crucifixion was for him an event of terrifying realism, regardless of time or place. This intensity is present even in some of the more exacting official commissions. For example, 'The Anatomy Lesson' (6) has a macabre inevitability in spite of the necessarily formal portrayal of the Doctor and his students.

For the art historian, Rembrandt's stature is not easy to assess and, in consequence, much sententious nonsense has been written by people completely out of touch with the emotional and physical struggle of drawing and painting. Rembrandt has no true roots in any great heterogeneous Romantic group; neither may he be neatly labelled as a 'stylist'. The achievements of the High Renaissance have no echo at all in his imagery. In 'Portrait of a Girl' (12) a simple moment in the life of a vital young woman is held and illumi-nated for always with a nobility utterly free of literary or social commentary. Where French and Italian painting of this period would have fallen into a sentimentally lyrical effusion, Rembrandt avoids the complaisant as well as the facile, and discovers an almost incorporeal mystery.

Especially in the genre paintings he sought the highest expression of a sentiment, of the situation and the people involved: a tree, an animal, a child, all have a separate and unique existence. Frequently in the Old Testament subjects too, he suggests 'the calm and the tempest' and thus reveals a tragic moment and a poignant gesture. In the 'David' (21) there is a passionately individual conception, as if the scene had been witnessed personally. Equally, he can reveal a great and gusty vulgarity as in 'Hendrickje' (10), and even combine this vital quality with a kind of grandeur as when he painted the realism of 'Saskia as Flora' (9). 'Bathsheba' (18) is real too, yet she is also the tender bulk of the peasant Hendrickje Stoffels.

All these are infinitely remote in emotional concept from the extravagant airs and graces of the school of his great contemporary Rubens—and even further removed from the grand mannerisms of Italy.

Rembrandt's people breathe the intimacy of everyday life. Two centuries later, when Delacroix wrote of some of the great Italians, and of Michelangelo in particular, he said: 'Michelangelo did not know one of the feelings of man, not one of his passions'. Outrageous as this sounds, it has a seed of truth; Rembrandt may unconsciously have acknowledged this, because in the comparative evaluation of all great painters, few display a stronger antipathy than he towards the misogyny and often mystical outlook of such giants of the classical tradition as Michelangelo or Leonardo.

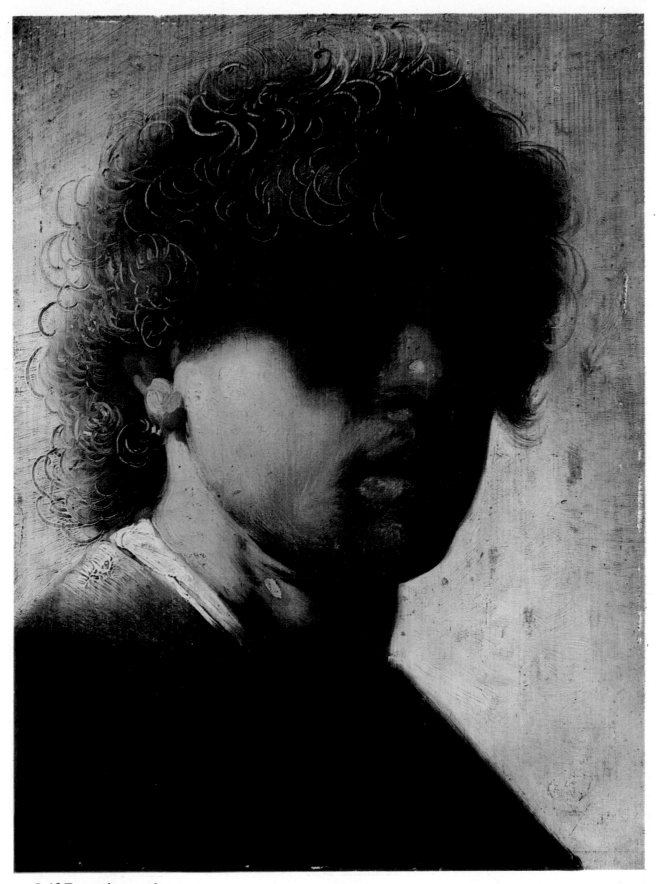

2. Self-Portrait, *c.* 1629
Oil on panel, 20 × 16 cm. Kassel, Staatliche Kunstsammlungen

3. A Scholar in a Lofty Interior, *c.* 1630
  Oil on panel, 55 × 46 cm. London, National Gallery

**4. Old Woman Reading (Rembrandt's Mother as the Prophetess Hannah), 1631**
Oil on panel, 60 × 48 cm. Amsterdam, Rijksmuseum

5. Simeon in the Temple (The Presentation in the Temple), 1631
Oil on panel, 61 × 48 cm. The Hague, Mauritshuis

6. The Anatomy Lesson of Professor Nicolaes Tulp, 1632
Oil on canvas, 162 × 216 cm. The Hague, Mauritshuis

7. Portrait of a Woman aged 83 years, 1634
Oil on panel, 68 × 53 cm. London, National Gallery

8. **Stormy Landscape**
Oil on panel, 52 × 72 cm. Brunswick, Herzog Anton Ulrich-Museum

9. Saskia as Flora, 1635
   Oil on panel, 121.5 × 96.5 cm. London, National Gallery

10. **Hendrickje Stoffels in Bed**, *c.* 1640
   Oil on canvas, 81 × 67 cm. Edinburgh, National Galleries of Scotland

11. Parade of the Civic Guard under Captain Frans Banning Cocq ('The Night Watch'), 1642
Oil on canvas, 387 × 502 cm. Amsterdam, Rijksmuseum

12. Portrait of a Girl leaning on the Lower Part of a Door, 1645
Oil on canvas, 100 × 84 cm. Chicago, Art Institute

**13. Self-Portrait, 1650**
Oil on canvas, 88 × 71 cm. Washington, National Gallery of Art: Widener Collection

14. Aristotle contemplating a Bust of Homer, 1653
Oil on canvas, 139 × 133 cm. New York, The Metropolitan Museum of Art

15. Old Man with Red Fur Cap in an Armchair, *c.* 1653
Oil on canvas, 51 × 37 cm. Berlin Dahlem, Staatliche Museen, Gemäldegalerie

16. A Woman Bathing, 1654
Oil on panel, 61 × 45 cm. London, National Gallery

17. The So-called 'Rembrandt's Brother' with a Helmet, 1654
Oil on canvas, 67 × 51 cm. Berlin Dahlem, Staatliche Museen, Gemäldegalerie

18. Bathsheba at her Toilet, 1654
   Oil on canvas, 142 × 142 cm. Paris, Louvre

19. The Slaughtered Ox, *c.* 1655
Oil on panel, 73 × 52 cm. Glasgow, Museums and Art Galleries

16. A Woman Bathing, 1654
Oil on panel, 61 × 45 cm. London, National Gallery

**17. The So-called 'Rembrandt's Brother' with a Helmet, 1654**
Oil on canvas, 67 × 51 cm. Berlin Dahlem, Staatliche Museen, Gemäldegalerie

20. The Descent from the Cross, 165(1)
Oil on canvas, 142 × 106 cm. Washington, National Gallery of Art: Widener Collection

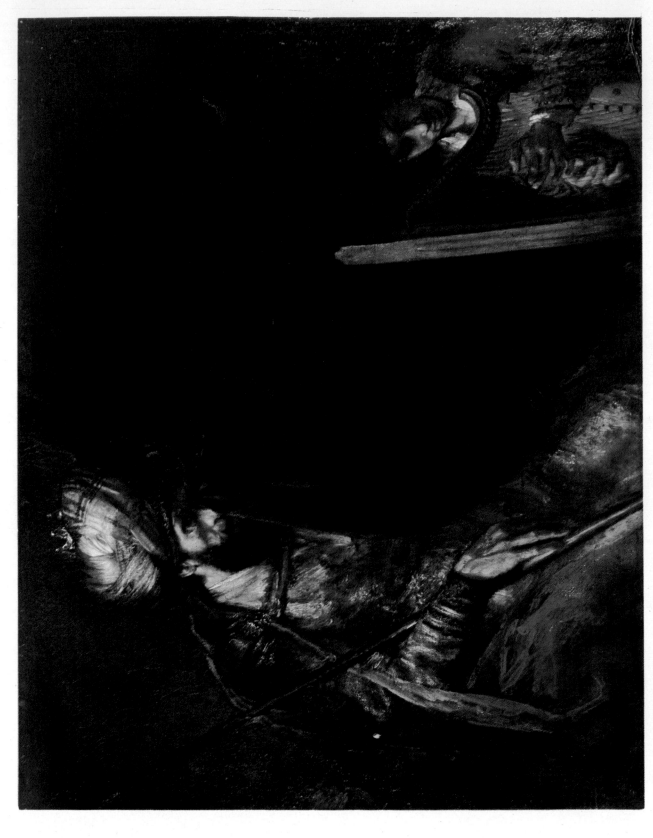

21. David harping before Saul, *c.* 1656
Oil on canvas, 130 × 164 cm. The Hague, Mauritshuis

22. Study of a Head, *c.* 1660/1
   Oil on panel, 23 × 19 cm. Washington, National Gallery of Art: Widener Collection

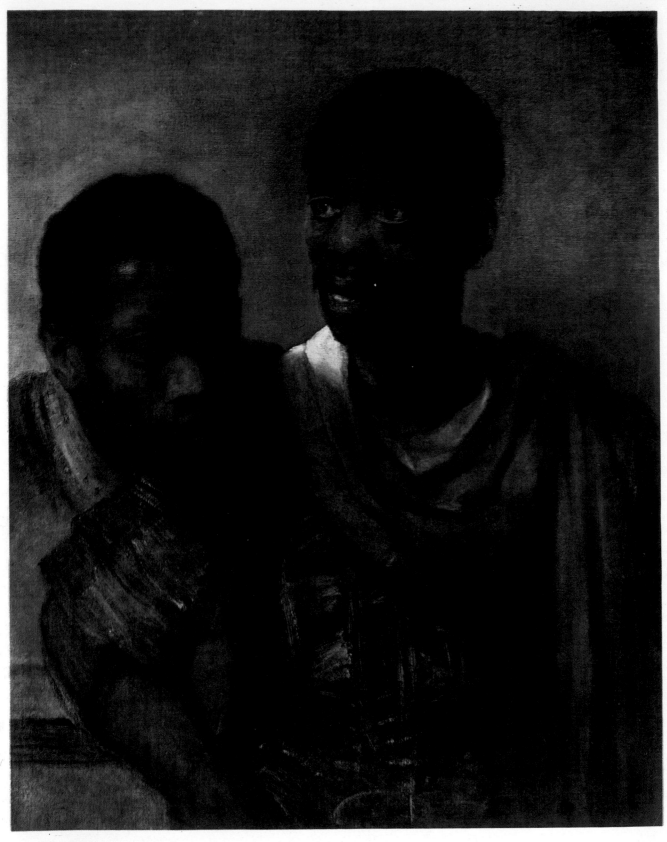

**23.** Two Negroes, 1661
Oil on canvas, 77×63 cm. The Hague, Mauritshuis

24. Portrait of a Married Couple (The Jewish Bride), *c.* 1665
Oil on canvas, 118 × 164 cm. Amsterdam, Rijksmuseum

25. Self-Portrait, *c.* 1668
  Oil on canvas, 114×97 cm. London, Kenwood House, Iveagh Bequest

# Drawings

Painters have rarely considered a drawing as an end in itself. It is the grand plan, the scaffolding or basic structure for the masses of tone and colour: it may be a kind of shorthand scribble or a laborious schematic layout, but seldom is a separate value attached to it other than as a means to an end.

In the twenty-seven drawings in this volume, one of the salient features of Rembrandt's draughtsmanship is emphasised—completeness. There is the conviction of a complete and economical statement in every subject. The range of his interest in everything happening about him in the house, on dykes and in town, was immense. A graphic record was almost part of his daily life—as it is with a good photographer today—and was by no means confined to providing the basis for paintings.

An essential part of Rembrandt's emotional reaction as a draughtsman from the moment he strikes a line, is an economy of means. In the 'Two Butchers '(33), drawn with great breadth on a small scale, a complete re-creation of the vigorous action is contrasted with the static carcass. The total effect has an almost sculptural dignity.

Or, for intensity of observation, few of his drawings can surpass 'Teaching a Child to Walk' (37 and 38). The sense of fleeting gesture and the anticipation of movement yet to come is rapidly touched in with a profound simplicity; there is the same brilliant sense of anticipated movement which Degas and Forain possessed to a high degree at the beginning of this century. This comparatively rare intuition owes nothing to 'style' or mere technical fireworks, but rather to the drawn line possessing a life of its own in time and space, lucid and never recondite in complex arabesque.

The technical means under Rembrandt's control vary little throughout his life. A hand-cut reed pen renders bulk and weight as he turns the blade of the nib; a brush line and tonal wash, sometimes emphasised with chalk, suggests a wide range of surface textures. The monumental 'Oriental' (29) and 'A Pregnant Woman' (31), both drawn in the 1630s, show little change in direct technical approach from the drawings of his last years—save perhaps an even greater economy of statement. Rembrandt is also able to combine what Ingres called 'des lignes, rien que des lignes' with rich shadow and apparent blaze of light retaining their separate qualities almost to the point of paradox.

Something of this effect can be seen in 'A Girl Sleeping' (49), interpreted in pulled brush lines and wash of great sympathy, which incidentally reveals an aspect of Rembrandt's appreciation of Oriental draughtsmen. This mature drawing and another study from about the same time, 'A Seated Female' (48), also reveal the results of his exploration of internal forms and their corresponding contours, their interdependence and the way in which they must be perfectly sustained to infer solidity. Whilst these two drawings possess a superb emotional intensity, their relatively small scale is no less remarkable, and supports the contention of those who insist that the majority of the world's great drawings are of modest dimensions. In fact, many of Rembrandt's finest drawings are easily contained within 10 × 8 inches. The little landscape drawings (46 and 47) for example, and the landscape etching (73), are 'life-size' in every way. They unfold with such economical skill that if only a few strokes were removed, much of the spaciousness would be lost.

This small selection from an enormous graphic *oeuvre* should be sufficient evidence of the vitality of an utterly individual language, free of specific mannerism and therefore immediate in impact.

26. Young Woman at her Toilet, *c.* 1632
   Pen and bistre, 238 × 184 mm. Vienna, Albertina

27. A Study of an Innkeeper, *c.* 1633
  Pen and ink, 177 × 140 mm. London, Victoria and Albert Museum

28. Rembrandt's Bride Saskia, 1633
Silverpoint, 185 × 107 mm. Berlin Dahlem, Staatliche Museen, Gemäldegalerie

29. An Oriental Standing, *c.* 1633
Pen and bistre, wash, 221 × 169 mm. London, British Museum

30. The Raising of the Cross, *c.* 1633
Black chalk, Indian ink, 232 × 187 mm. Vienna, Albertina

31. A Pregnant Woman Standing, *c.* 1633
Pen and bistre, 164 × 110 mm. London, British Museum

**32. A Woman Standing with a Candle, 1635**
Pen with bistre and Indian ink, 181 × 132 mm. London, British Museum

**33. Two Butchers at Work, 1635**
Pen and bistre, 149 × 200 mm. Frankfurt, Städelsches Kunstinstitut

**34. Saskia carrying Rumbertus downstairs, 1636**
Pen and bistre, 185 × 133 mm. New York, Pierpoint Morgan Library

**35.** Female Nude with a Snake (probably 'Cleopatra'), *c.* 1637
Red chalk, 245 × 140 mm. London, Villiers David

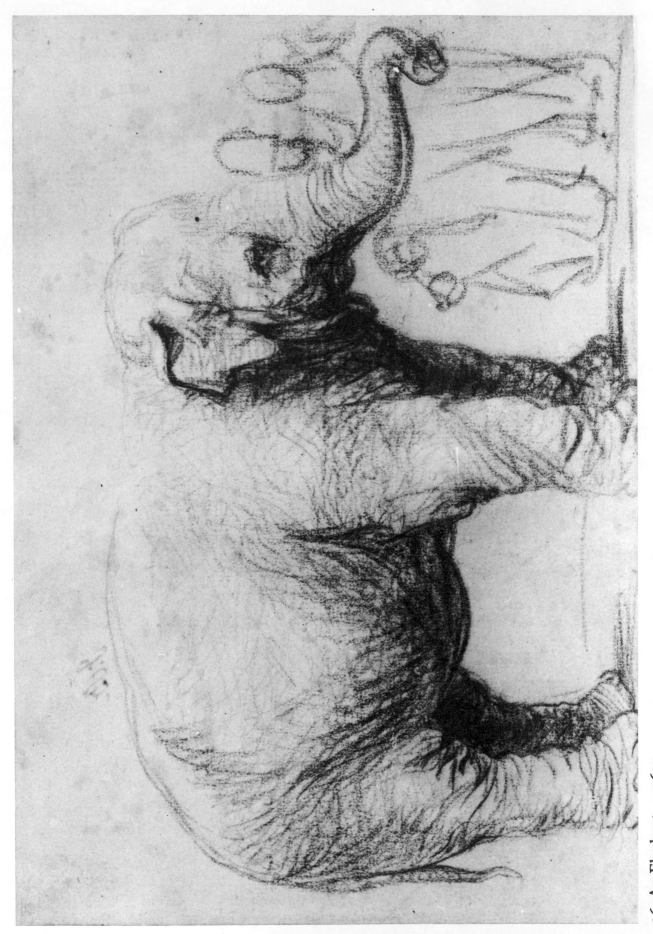

36. An Elephant, c. 1637
Black chalk, 178×256 mm. London, British Museum

**37. Two Women teaching a Child to Walk,** *c.* 1637
Chalk, 103 × 128 mm. London, British Museum

**38. Woman teaching child to Walk,** *c.* 1646
Pen and bistre, 165 × 160 mm. Stockholm, Nationalmuseum

39. A Lioness eating a Bird, c. 1641
Black chalk, wash Indian ink, 127×240 mm. London, British Museum

**40. Three Studies of an Old Man, *c.* 1643**
Pen, wash in bistre and Indian ink, 150 × 184 mm. London, British Museum

**41. A Bearded Old Man, *c.* 1641**
Pen and bistre, 111 × 57 mm.
London, British Museum

**42. A Man with a Wooden Leg, *c.* 1647**
Black chalk, 143 × 90 mm. Vienna, Albertina

43. Christ Preaching (the basis of The Hundred Guilder Print), *c.* 1643
Pen and bistre, 198 × 230 mm. Paris, Louvre, Rothschild Collection

44. The Good Samaritan, *c.* 1643
Pen and bistre, 184×287 mm. London, British Museum

45. Study for the Figure of Susanna, *c.* 1647
Black chalk, 203 × 164 mm. Berlin Dahlem, Staatliche Museen, Gemäldegalerie

**46. A Road passing an Inn,** *c.* 1653
Pen and Wash, 111 × 172 mm. London, British Museum

**47. A Little Inn and Huts,** *c.* 1653
Pen and bistre, 129 × 178 mm. Groningen, Groniger Museum

48. A Seated Female Nude wearing a Straw Hat, *c.* 1654/6
Pen and wash, 263×200 mm. London, Victoria and Albert Museum, Dyce Collection

**49. A Girl Sleeping. Hendrickje,** *c.* 1655/6
Brush, bistre wash, 245×203 mm. London, British Museum

50. A Woman looking out of a Window, *c.* 1656
Pen and brush, 292×162 mm. Paris, Louvre

*Joseph a le soin des prisonniers et les console* 171

**51. Joseph waiting on his Two Fellow Prisoners,** *c.* 1656
Pen and bistre, 180 × 194 mm. London, British Museum

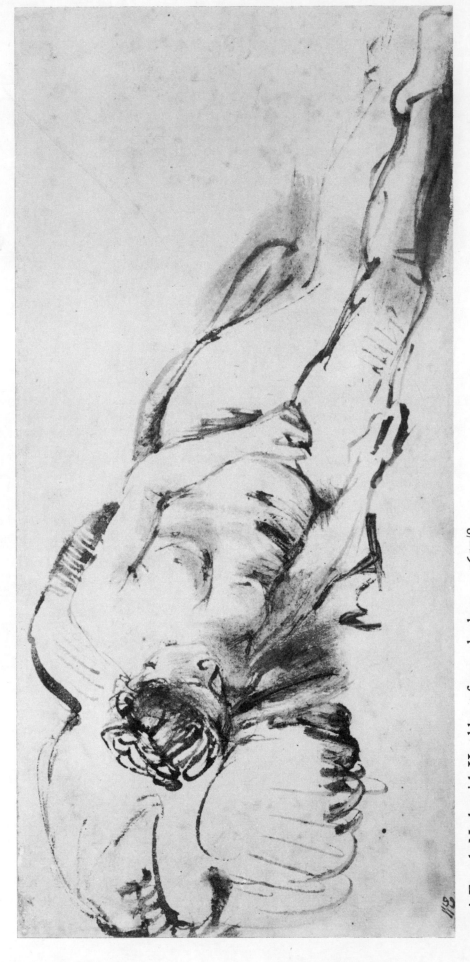

52. A Female Nude with Head bent forward asleep, c. 1657/8
Pen and bistre, 135 × 283 mm. Amsterdam, Rijksmuseum

# Etchings

More than a hundred years elapsed between one of the earliest essays in etching—Dürer's 'Cannon' in the first quarter of the sixteenth century—and the tremendous exploitation of the medium by Rembrandt.

In his early years Rembrandt had little access to the work of any forerunners of importance in the process, or indeed to little worth-while advice on which to base his technique.

The first print in this selection, 'An Old Beggar Woman' (53), is from a large and more or less continuous series of beggars and pedlars which he expanded in different forms for about thirty years. It was a vital aspect of humanity to him, yet these rugged prints, of the early years especially, have been considered almost as side-tracks by many critics who were apparently unable to appreciate such magnificent conceptions as the 'Beggar' (54) or the 'Beggar Man and Woman' (55). Equally, there has been extravagant and un-critical appraisal of Rembrandt's entire etched work, making it an object of ridiculous worship, while his creative impulse in the medium has been all too neatly divided into three compartments. In fact, his development as an etcher was on such broad terms as to defy arbitrary classification.

From about the age of thirty until the last few years of his life he exploited tonal etching and the technique of a free, running line comparatively constantly in both figure subjects and landscapes. 'The Beggar' (60), from about 1630, has an affinity in linear freedom with the beautiful open drawing in the tragic 'Tobit' (76), more than twenty years later—just as some of the late plates of great tonal richness are frequently anticipated in his early designs.

Perhaps one positive feature in his development is an early realisation of the natural scale of an etched subject.

Because of the unique effect a needle-drawn line may yield when carefully etched, Rembrandt was able to achieve both delicacy and breadth of treatment often on extremely small plates: 'Rembrandt's Mother' (58) and the 'Three Heads' (65) are fine examples. His perception of the medium's purely graphic immediacy is also vividly seen in such plates as 'The Flute Player' (66), or in the later 'Landscape' (73).

He also introduced drypoint into some of the later designs, as both a reinforcement of the tonal scheme and a contrast-ing quality in itself. Many of these passages in the more elaborate plates are far from successful, although 'Arnold Tholinx' (79) is a magnificent exception.

Naturally, whilst they are best appreciated in the original, the nobility of intention alone makes 'The Three Crosses' (77) one of the most monumental plates in the history of the medium, and the smaller 'Descent from the Cross' (78), with its quieter horror and primitive simplicity, shows an aspect of Rembrandt that has had considerable influence on later generations of etchers in their use of drypoint.

Rembrandt was constantly experimenting with slashing graver and needle lines, often raising a heavy burr on top of already over-etched and collapsed areas of metal. The reasons are not always as obvious as they appear. In all probability, his frequent illnesses and weak eyesight of later years made him resort to a quick method of producing the rich tones so typical of the newly discovered 'mezzotint'. There is, how-ever, no evidence that he used this discovery, and no etchings appear to have been made during the last eight years of his life.

Nevertheless we can be grateful for the rich legacy of at least three hundred authentic prints from his own hand, prints which tell their own story.

**53. Old Beggar Woman,** *c.* 1629
102 × 45 mm. London, British Museum

**54. Beggar with a Stick,** *c.* 1629
97 × 42 mm. London, British Museum

**55. Beggar Man and Woman behind a Bank,** *c.* 1629
116 × 84 mm. London, British Museum

56. The Small Lion Hunt (two lions), *c.* 1629
154 × 121 mm. London, British Museum

**57. Rembrandt Open-mouthed, *c.* 1630**
73 × 62 mm. London, British Museum

**58. Rembrandt's Mother, 1628**
66 × 63 mm. London, British Museum

**59. A Bald-headed Man (Rembrandt's Father?), 1630**
118 × 97 mm. London, British Museum

60. A Beggar in a High Cap, standing and leaning on a Stick, *c.* 1630
156 × 120 mm. London, British Museum

**61. Rembrandt's Mother in Oriental Headdress, 1631**
145 × 129 mm. London, British Museum

62. The Fourth Oriental Head, *c.* 1635
158 × 135 mm. London, British Museum

63. Girl with Hair falling on her Shoulders, *c.* 1635
220 × 168 mm. London, British Museum

**64. Studies of the Head of Saskia and Others, 1636**
151 × 127 mm. London, British Museum

**65. Three Heads of Women: one asleep, 1637**
142×97 mm. London, British Museum

**66. The Flute Player, 1642**
115 × 143 mm. London, British Museum

**67. A Cottage with a White Paling, *c.* 1642/3**
130 × 158 mm. London, British Museum

68. Christ with the Sick. The Hundred Guilder Print, c. 1643
278×386 mm. London, British Museum

**69. The Hog, 1643**
143 × 187 mm. London, British Museum

**70. Study from the Nude: a man seated on the ground with one leg extended, 1646**
166 × 97 mm. London, British Museum

71. The Omval (with lovers in the shade of a tree), 1645
185 × 225 mm. London, British Museum

72. Jews in a Synagogue (Judas?), 1648
71 × 129 mm. London, British Museum

73. Landscape with a Sportsman and Dogs, 1652
129 × 157 mm. Cambridge, Fitzwilliam Museum

74. Beggars receiving Alms at the Door of a House, 1648
164 × 128 mm. London, British Museum

75. Landscape with Three Gabled Cottages beside a Road, 1650
161 × 202 mm. Cambridge, Fitzwilliam Museum

76. The Blindness of Tobit, 1651
161 × 129 mm. London, British Museum

77. The Three Crosses, 1653
387 × 450 mm. London, British Museum

78. The Descent from The Cross, by torchlight, 1654

204 × 161 mm. London, British Museum

79. Arnold Tholinx, Portrait, *c.* 1655/6
173 × 149 mm. London, British Museum

80. Christ Preaching. 'La Petite Tombe', 1656
155×207 mm. London, British Museum

81. Jupiter and Antiope, 1659
139×205 mm. Vienna, Albertina

# Acknowledgements

The publishers wish to thank the following for permission to reproduce the works and for supplying material from which the reproductions have been made.

Amsterdam, Rijksmuseum: 4, 11, 24, 52
Berlin Dahlem, Staatliche Museen, Gemäldegalerie: 15, 17, 28, 45
Brunswick, Herzog Anton Ulrich-Museum: 8
Cambridge, the Syndics of the Fitzwilliam Museum: 73, 75
Chicago, The Art Institute: 12
Edinburgh, National Galleries of Scotland: 10
Frankfurt, Städelsches Kunstinstitut: 33
Glasgow, Museums and Art Galleries: 19
Groningen, Groninger Museum: 47
The Hague, Mauritshuis: 5, 6, 21, 23
Kassel, Staatliche Kunstammlungen: 2
London, The Trustees of the British Museum: 29, 31, 32, 36, 37, 39, 40, 41, 44, 46,
    49, 51, 53, 54, 55, 56, 57, 58, 59, 60, 61, 62, 63, 64, 65, 66, 67, 68, 69, 70, 71, 72,
    74, 76, 77, 78, 79, 80
  Mr Villiers David: 35
  London County Council, the Iveagh Bequest, Kenwood: 25
  The Trustees of the National Gallery: 3, 7, 9, 16
  Victoria & Albert Museum: 27, 48 (Dyce Collection)
New York, The Metropolitan Museum of Art: 14
  The Pierpont Morgan Library: 34
Paris, Bibliothèque Nationale: 1
  Louvre; 18, 50, 43 (Rothschild Collection)
Stockholm, Nationalmuseum: 38
Vienna, Albertina: 26, 30, 42, 81
Washington, D.C., National Gallery of Art, Widener Collection: 13, 20, 22